RESEARCH TOOL KIT

COLLECT
YOUR
THOUGHTS

Organizing Information

by Jennifer Fandel

Consultant:
Gwen Hart, PhD
Assistant Professor of English Composition
Buena Vista University
Storm Lake, Iowa

CAPSTONE PRESS
a capstone imprint

Fact Finders are published by Capstone Press,
1710 Roe Crest Drive, North Mankato, Minnesota 56003.
www.capstonepub.com

Library of Congress Cataloging-in-Publication Data
Fandel, Jennifer.
 Collect your thoughts : organizing information / by Jennifer Fandel.
   p. cm.
 Includes bibliographical references and index.
 Summary: "Explores ways to organize information when doing research and writing
reports and other written materials"—Provided by publisher.
 ISBN 978-1-4296-9948-8 (library binding)
 ISBN 978-1-62065-786-7 (paperback)
 ISBN 978-1-4765-1568-7 (ebook PDF)
1. Research—Juvenile literature. 2. Report writing—Juvenile literature. I. Title.
LB1047.3.F36 2013
 371.30281—dc23   2012034015

Editorial Credits
Jill Kalz, editor; Juliette Peters, designer; Eric Manske, production specialist

Photo Credits
Alamy: AHowden, 10; Corbis: Bettmann, 6; Dreamstime: Pressureua, 4; Shutterstock:
bogdan ionescu, 5, Eric Isselée, 22, Fotoline, 14, Irina oxilixo Danilova, 21 (retriever),
jcjgphotography, 16, Lisa A. Svara, 23, MisterElements, cover, monbibi, 7, phloxii, 21
(chihuahua), Robert Adrian Hillman, 28 (silhouette), Robert Kneschke, 12, Sally Scott,
19 (artichoke), SmileStudio, 26-27 (notebook), Tiplyashin Anatoly, 19 (pineapple),
Vulkanette, 15, Wendy Farrington, 28-29; Wikimedia: Joyce N. Boghosian, White House
photographer, 9

Artistic Effects
Shutterstock: blue67design, Erica Truex, MisterElements

Printed in the United States of America in Stevens Point, Wisconsin.
082013   007683R

TABLE OF CONTENTS

Collect, Organize, and Share

The clock's ticking. You have an assignment and a deadline. Stacks of books, magazines, and website printouts cover your desk. But how do you make sense of this information? And how do you turn it all into a report, speech, or blog?

KEEPING YOUR INFORMATION ORGANIZED IS THE KEY.

Think of research as a puzzle. When you work on a puzzle, you group the same colors together. You connect all of the straight edges and make a frame. Organizing your research isn't much different. This book shows you how to sort through your research puzzle pieces. It gives tips on how to group them. And in the end, it'll help you turn your research into one whole, beautiful picture.

CHAPTER ONE

Making a Plan

Preparation: Purpose First

What is the **purpose** of your research? Figure this out before you read or take notes. It will keep you from doing too much or too little research. It helps you stay on **topic**.

The purpose tells you what kind of research you need to do. Is your assignment a biography or descriptive **essay**? A report or an opinion essay? A biography is the story of someone's life, from the beginning to the end. A descriptive essay helps readers picture something. You explain facts and details in a report. An opinion essay is filled with facts that support your view on a subject.

Write a short <u>biography</u> of Martin Luther King Jr.

Write an essay <u>describing</u> four paintings of Pablo Picasso.

Write a report <u>explaining</u> the difference between the lives of queen bees and drones.

Write an <u>opinion</u> essay on who should be the next president of the United States.

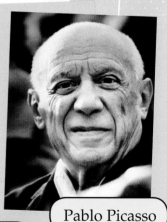

Pablo Picasso

purpose—the reason behind your writing
topic—what your writing is about
essay—the name given for a short paper on a theme

WHO, WHAT, WHEN, WHERE, WHY, and HOW

When doing research, remember these six question words. They are a good starting point for your research. They'll help ensure you include all the background research your audience needs.

ACTIVITY: ASK AND ANSWER

Write down your assignment. Circle the word or phrase that shows the purpose of your research. Now list all of the questions you need to answer. Come back to this list of questions throughout your research. Make sure you find all of the information you need.

Example: Explain the process of a volcanic eruption.

<u>Who</u> has seen volcanoes erupt?
Are there volcano experts?
Who are they?

<u>What</u> are the layers of Earth like under a volcano?

<u>When</u> do volcanoes erupt?

<u>Where</u> do volcanoes erupt?

<u>Why</u> do volcanoes erupt?

<u>How</u> does it happen?

Should I Quote or Summarize?

When taking notes, you can **summarize** or **quote** the information. To summarize, put the facts, details, and ideas into your own words. Read the information carefully. Think about it. Then, without looking at the source, write down what was said. After you've written this note, reread your source. Did you capture the fact or idea correctly? Make sure you didn't use any phrases that appear in the source. That's **plagiarism**. Your summary should state—in a new and different way—what your source says.

Quotations are phrases, sentences, and sometimes paragraphs that belong to someone else. They must be written exactly as they appear in your source. When you take notes, place the quoted material inside quotation marks. Also add the label *(quote)* before the quotation.

Whether summarizing or quoting, be clear that the idea is coming from another source.

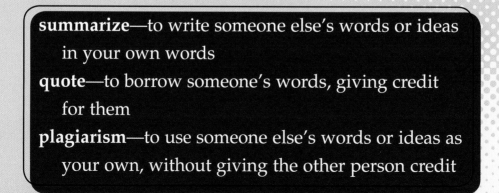

summarize—to write someone else's words or ideas in your own words

quote—to borrow someone's words, giving credit for them

plagiarism—to use someone else's words or ideas as your own, without giving the other person credit

Read the paragraph below. Then summarize it. Next have a friend read the paragraph and write a summary. Exchange summaries and see how they compare. How are your summaries similar? Different?

Michelle Obama is one of many American first ladies who has stood up for a cause during her husband's presidency. She worked as a lawyer before her time in the White House. She was concerned about the obesity problems in the United States and developed programs to get kids exercising and eating right. She even planted a vegetable garden on the White House lawn to show people how fun and easy good nutrition can be. When Hillary Rodham Clinton was first lady, she tried to get laws passed to give health care coverage to everyone in the United States. Ms. Clinton was a lawyer and used the skills and training from her work. First Lady Laura Bush was a librarian. In her time in the White House, she encouraged more young people to read.

Michelle Obama

Quote Me on This

Always summarize more than you quote. People want to read *your* words and hear *your* voice. Think of quotations as cymbals in a marching band. They give an added oomph to your writing if placed in the right spot. But if they're crashing all the time, the band won't sound so great.

Remember, it's your job to make the information clear to your audience. If you don't understand an idea or fact, your readers might not understand it either. If there's something you don't understand, ask someone to help you make sense of it. Look up unknown terms in a dictionary or encyclopedia.

WHEN TO QUOTE AND WHEN TO SUMMARIZE

 Is this a fact that can be found in many sources?

> Earth and the other planets in our solar system orbit the sun.

Yes, summarize.   **No, quote.**

 Can I explain this information in my own words?

> The astronomer Nicolaus Copernicus stated that Earth and the planets revolve around the sun. This was in the 1500s, and most people did not believe him.

Yes, summarize.   **No, quote.**

Does the information contain a special idea or term that belongs to someone else?

> Copernican heliocentricism (definition): "From helio, meaning sun; and centric, meaning center. The term is used to describe Nicolaus Copernicus' breakthrough theory that the sun was the center of the solar system." From *The Dictionary of Science Terms*

Yes, quote.   No, summarize.

 Would using the words of the author, expert, or speaker support your ideas better?

> Mary Sunshine, president of the Copernicus Learning Lab in Washington, D.C., states: "Copernicus made people think differently about the world and themselves. If someone tells you that you're not the center of attention anymore, you're not happy about that. People didn't want to believe that they weren't at the center of the solar system. It took away their feeling of power."

Yes, quote.   No, summarize.

THE IMPORTANCE OF AUDIENCE

The people you write for are your audience. Let's say you need to give a speech to the Iguana Owners Club. These people know a lot about iguanas, so you can use special iguana terms, such as "parietal eye." But what if you're writing to the local newspaper? Your words would be different, because the audience is different. You would need to explain more general information about iguanas, since most readers wouldn't know much about them.

CHAPTER TWO

Note-Taking: Dive In!

Mark Your Trail: Source Information

Park workers often mark trails with signs or arrows. The markers keep hikers from getting lost. You need to do the same thing when taking notes. If something in your notes confuses you later, you have to be able to go back to the source quickly.

When you use a source, write down important information about it right away. Not only will this info help clear up any confusion later, it will also help you create a **bibliography** at the end of your research. For books, the markers are simple. Most books have authors and page numbers. But what about websites, **podcasts**, movies, or TV shows? Most don't list an author's name, and they definitely don't have page numbers. What markers do you use? The following chart will help.

bibliography—the list of sources you used in your research

podcast—a program that can be listened to on a computer or other media player

Information needed for each source

	Books	Magazines	Websites	Podcasts	Movies	TV Shows	Interviews You Conducted
Author	Yes	Yes, if available	Yes, if available	No	No	No	No
Article Title	No	Yes	Yes, if available	Yes. It's the name given to the episode.	No	Yes. It's the name given to the episode.	No
Source Title	Yes	Yes	Yes. This is the website name.	Yes. This is the program name.	Yes	Yes. This is the program name.	Yes. Title it "Interview with (insert name)."
Publisher's Location	Yes	No	Yes. This is the website address.	No	No	No	No
Publisher's Name	Yes	No	No	No	No	No	No
Date of Publication	Yes	Yes. This could be a date or volume number.	Yes. This is the copyright or date when the site was last modified.	Yes. This is when the podcast was first broadcast.	Yes. This is the copyright year or the release date.	Yes. This is the date when the program was first broadcast.	No
Access Date	No	No	Yes. This is when you found this information.	No	No	No	Yes. This is when you did the interview.
Page Number	Yes	Yes	No	No	No	No	No

Note by Note

You've got 20 note cards of information, but you forgot to write down your sources. And your handwriting's a mess. Ugh! No one likes to start over, especially on a research project. For every note make sure that you record enough information to lead you back to your source. And be neat about it! Place your source information at the top of your note card or to the left of each note. Make it your first step. Then you won't forget it.

LET'S TAKE A LOOK AT NOTES FOR VARIOUS SOURCES.

If you have two authors with the same last name, use the initial of each author's first name in your notes.

- D. Pierce, 44 — drones live about 90 days
  (from "Drones" in *Bee Magazine* by Diane Pierce)

- V. Pierce, 53 — queens may lay 2,000 eggs in a day
  (from *Bee Royalty* by Virgil Pierce)

For two books by the same author, use the first word of the title in your notes. If the first word is *A*, *An*, or *The*, move to the second word.

- Brown, *Sweetest*, 34 — usually just one queen bee per hive
  (from *The Sweetest Honey* by Ann Brown)

- Brown, *Wonder*, 15 — drones are male honey bees
  (from *Wonder Bees* by Ann Brown)

If you've used two episodes in the same podcast or program, such as *The Science News* podcast, use the episode title in your notes.

- "Life in the Hives"— drones do not gather food and do no work within the hive

- "Bee Days"— drones don't have stingers, so they cannot defend the hive

ACTIVITY: KEEP TRACK

Make a two-column research log. You can do this either in a notebook or on a computer. In the left-hand column, write your summary or quotation. In the right-hand column, write the research question that your information answers. The log will help keep you on track as you look through sources and take notes.

Information	Question
Most volcanoes form along the edges of tectonic plates. About 75 percent of Earth's active volcanoes lie along a tectonic plate in the Pacific Ocean. They make up the Ring of Fire.	Where do volcanoes erupt?
Volcanoes usually give some type of warning before erupting: earthquake, blasts of steam, change in ground temperature.	When do volcanoes erupt?

Neat and Clean Notes

Notes have to be neatly written or typed. You don't want to waste time guessing what you wrote, and you don't want to re-read your sources. But notes don't have to be full sentences. In fact, notes don't even have to be full words. When you're doing research, saving even a little time is a good thing. The key is creating a system and sticking to it. Then you never have to guess again.

NOTE-TAKER TIPS

A, An, and The usually do not need to be written.

A dash can be used for definitions. Pink Lady—type of apple.

Often people use abbreviations, such as b. for born and d. for died.

Also, to avoid writing terms over and over again, you can abbreviate them. Theory of relativity could be Th of rel.

A dash is usually used to indicate a range of dates, such as 1256–1300.

Quotations break the "no full sentence" rule. They should always appear in your notes exactly as they appear in the source. Sometimes an author will quote someone else. If you want to use this quote, you need to make sure that readers know who wrote or spoke the quote. For example, Matilda Birdsong wrote a book on endangered birds. In the book she quoted a speech by Sally Eagle, a specialist in bird habitats. Your notes need to name the book the information came from. But readers need to know that the quote came from Sally Eagle, rather than the author Matilda Birdsong.

Birdsong, 44—(quote) Sally Eagle said: "If we destroy the places where birds live, we hurt the birds. That's often why they become extinct."

ADD PUNCH!

Quotations add extra punch to your writing. They can capture a speaker's personality. This is helpful when writing a biography or showing an emotional event. Quotations from experts can also add strong support for your ideas. Experts have studied their subject for a long time. There's a lot of knowledge packed in their words.

CHAPTER THREE

Sort It Out

Groups and Labels

Labels help you sort your information. Look at the list of questions you plan to answer in your research paper. Now group the related questions together. Finally, find a word to sum up each group. These words are the labels you'll add to your notes.

For example, for a biography of Martin Luther King Jr., you might want to know the following: When was he born? Where was he born? Who were his parents? What was his childhood like? Where did the family live? What childhood experiences shaped him? What experiences did he have as an adult?

Grouping and labeling the questions might look like this:

When was he born?

Where was he born? = **BIRTH**

Who were his parents?

What was his childhood like?

Where did the family live? = **CHILDHOOD**

What childhood experiences shaped him?

What experiences did he have as an adult? = **INFLUENCES**

If every note has a label, you can find and group your information easily. If you use note cards, you can place all of the note cards with the same labels together. If you take notes in a notebook, try highlighting your labels with different colors. That will make it easier to group your information. If you use a computer, cut and paste. Put all information with the same label on the same page together.

ACTIVITY: GET A GROUP

Compare and contrast pineapples and artichokes. Look at the picture of each one, and then make a list of 20 questions about them. Next group similar questions together. Finally, label the groups.

Sample questions and labels:
What do the leaves look like?
(label: OUTSIDE DESCRIPTION)
How does the fruit taste?
(label: TASTE)
Where do they grow?
(label: CLIMATE)

Idea Webs and Thesis Statements

You've seen a spider web before, right? How the strands connect to one another? Idea webs show you how your research fits together. If you can't connect a piece of information to one of your main ideas or supporting ideas, it tells you something. The information might not fit.

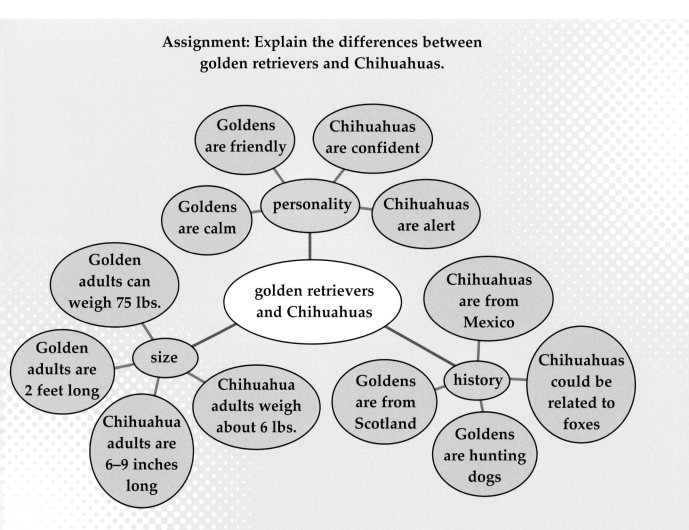

Assignment: Explain the differences between golden retrievers and Chihuahuas.

When your idea web is complete, you can create your thesis statement. Your thesis statement should be a clear answer to your assignment. Most thesis statements say what you will do in your paper. They also say how you will prove this.

Assignment: Explain the differences between golden retrievers and Chihuahuas.

Thesis #1: Golden retrievers and Chihuahuas are dogs that a lot of people like.

Is this what the assignment asked? Not really. Give it another try. Hint: Look at the circles that support your topic in your idea web.

~~**Thesis #1:** Golden retrievers and Chihuahuas are dogs that a lot of people like.~~

Thesis #2: Golden retrievers and Chihuahuas are different in size, personality, and history.

Does this thesis match up to what the assignment asks? Are the supporting ideas clear? If so, you're getting closer to writing your paper.

Outlines: Choosing Your Best Information

Outlines are similar to idea webs. Both of them help you figure out the order of your information. But outlines are often more detailed. Try creating an outline after you make an idea web.

Information can be arranged in all kinds of ways. Writing a biography? Your outline should show that you're telling a life story from the beginning to the end. Writing a process paper? Information should be presented in the same order as the steps you would take.

At the top of the page, write your thesis statement. Below that list your main points with capital letters. Your supporting points will go under each of your main points and should be numbered. Putting information in order gives you structure. It's like having a blueprint for your research paper.

Thesis: Golden retrievers and Chihuahuas are different in size, personality, and history.

A. Size
    1. Weight and height of Chihuahua
    2. Weight and height of golden retriever
B. Personality
    1. Chihuahua confident and alert
    2. Golden retriever friendly and calm
C. History
    1. Chihuahua related to foxes
    2. Chihuahua from Mexico
    3. Golden retriever a hunting dog
    4. Golden retriever from Scotland

After you finish your outline, look back on your notes. Put your note cards in the order the information will be used in your paper. If you took notes in a notebook, highlight the main points in the outline to match the color of the labeled notes. If you used a computer, cut and paste the information into a computer outline.

CHAPTER FOUR

Are You Ready to Write?

Bibliography: Put Your Sources in Order

Imagine this: Your classmates like your paper so much that they want to know more. (Hey, it could happen!) That's why you need a bibliography. A bibliography is an alphabetical list of sources that you used to write your paper. It's usually placed at the end of your paper.

The information in your bibliography is like a trail of breadcrumbs. It takes readers right back to the library shelf, website, or person you interviewed.

Most book sources in a bibliography look like this:

Fandel, Jennifer. *Collect Your Thoughts: Organizing Information.* North Mankato, Minn.: Capstone Press, 2013.

For magazines, put the article title in quotation marks before the magazine name.

Schnorr, Jackie. "Loud Noises in the Night." *Sleep Magazine.* 22 July 2012: 30–32.

For podcasts and TV shows, there's usually no author. The date is when the podcast was accessed or when the TV program aired.

"Zombie Choir." *Make a Noise.* Travel Channel. 14 Aug. 2012.

Websites usually don't have an author either. They may have article titles or page names. The key piece of information is the Web address.

"Biography: J. Patrick Lewis." *The Poetry Foundation Website.* www.poetryfoundation.org/bio/j-patrick-lewis#poet. Accessed 12 March 2013.

Include any interviews too. You need to list who you interviewed and when the interview took place. Note if it was a telephone, e-mail, or face-to-face interview.

Clinton, Bill. Telephone interview. 20 Jan. 2012.

BIBLIOGRAPHY RULES!

1. When you alphabetize your sources, use the first word for each source. If the word is *A*, *An*, or *The*, move to the second word.

2. Most bibliographies use a hanging indent. If information for one of your entries flows onto a second line, indent the second line.

3. Always check with your teacher about the bibliography format. Styles differ.

Check Your Checklist

Use this checklist for every paper you write.

Preparation

✓ Did you review your assignment and create a list of questions you need to answer in your paper?

✓ Do all of the questions match your assignment?

If anything doesn't match up, fix the problems now.

Note-Taking Review

✓ Are you missing any author names or page numbers?

✓ Are any of your quotations unclear or missing quotation marks?

✓ Are you missing the names of any people that you've quoted?

✓ Are any of your summaries unclear?

✓ Are any of your notes missing information to trace it back to the source?

If there is anything missing, fix the problems now.

Sorting Review

✓ Look back at the list of your preparation questions. Are they grouped together and labeled? Do they match up to the notes you've taken?

✓ Are all notes labeled with the correct subject?

✓ If you used note cards, are all note cards with similar labels grouped together?

✓ If you used a notebook, did you highlight each of your labels with a different color? Or did you find another way to group your information together?

✓ If you used a computer, did you cut and paste your notes with similar subjects on the same page?

If there is anything missing, fix the problems now.

Organizing Review

✓ Do all of your ideas fit in your idea web? If not, do you need to revise that idea? Or does that idea need to be left out?

✓ Did you create a thesis statement that answers your assignment?

✓ Do your supporting ideas appear in your thesis?

✓ Did you create an outline with supporting points?

✓ Are the ideas in your outline in the same order that they will be in your paper?

✓ Will the support make sense to your audience?

Once you've fixed all problems,

YOU ARE READY TO WRITE!

Enjoy the Ride

Researching and writing are processes filled with twists and turns. They're not merry-go-rounds; they're roller coasters. You're constantly learning new things, and you need to think about how to keep from flying out of your seat!

To better enjoy the ride, get organized. The more organized your research is, the easier your writing task will be. Make sure you understand the assignment. Prepare for the task with a list of questions. Take good notes with a clear trail back to the source, and sort your notes. Use idea webs and outlines to make the writing task easier.

Buckle up, and get ready to write!

GLOSSARY

bibliography (bib-lee-OG-ruh-fee)—an alphabetical list of the sources used in a research paper or project

essay (ES-ay)—a piece of writing that gives the author's opinion on a particular subject

plagiarism (PLAY-juh-riz-uhm)—copying someone else's work and passing it off as your own

podcast (POD-kast)—a program that can be listened to on a computer or other media player

purpose (PUR-pus)—the reason for which something is made or done

quote (KWOHT)—to borrow someone's words, giving credit for them

summarize (SUH-muh-rize)—to give a shortened account of something using only the main points

topic (TAH-pik)—what something is about; a subject

READ MORE

Bentley, Nancy. *Don't Be a Copycat!: Write a Great Report Without Plagiarizing.* Berkeley Heights, N.J.: Enslow Elementary, 2008.

Gaines, Ann Graham. *Ace Your Research Paper.* Ace It! Information Literacy Series. Berkeley Heights, N.J.: Enslow Publishers, 2009.

Mack, James. *Write for Success.* Life Skills. Chicago: Heinemann Library, 2009.

Somervill, Barbara A. *Written Reports.* School Projects Survival Guides. Chicago: Heinemann Library, 2009.

INTERNET SITES

FactHound offers a safe, fun way to find Internet sites related to this book. All of the sites on FactHound have been researched by our staff.

Here's all you do:

Visit *www.facthound.com*

Type in this code: 9781429699488

Check out projects, games and lots more at
www.capstonekids.com

INDEX